GW00468923

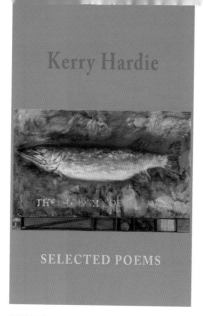

# KERRY HARDIE
## Selected Poems

Kerry Hardie is one of Ireland's leading poets. Her *Selected Poems* covers work written over two decades and draws on five collections. Her poetry questions, celebrates and challenges all aspects of life and experience, but ultimately is concerned with the quiet realisation that 'there is nothing to do in the world except live in it'.

A number of her poems are narratives or parables in which experience yields a spiritual lesson and consolation; others chart a coming to terms with death or illness and an acceptance of inevitability or flux. Human life quivers in consort with other lives in these seasons of the heart.

'The essence of her marvellous poems lies in the way she sees through a material world that is rendered truthfully, plainly yet freshly'
– GEORGE SZIRTES, *Irish Times*

February 2011    £9.95 paper    (Bloodaxe)
978 1 85224 890 1    104 pages    216 x 138mm
*Ireland:* Gallery Press (US rights reserved)

**KERRY HARDIE** has published five collections with Gallery Press in Ireland and two novels with HarperCollins. Her many prizes include the Michael Hartnett Award for Poetry in 2005. She lives in County Kilkenny.

**Only This Room**, by Kerry Hardie (Gallery Press, £10.95) *Eire.*

*RP? March*
*= 0/0 April.*

Sparse, open, trusting to plainness, deceptively clear and direct, Hardie's collection can conjure a scene in very few words. Take the haunting sequence "The Red Window", which measures gradually changing skies viewed from a single room - "that morning you wake / to find the red window / is full up with weather." The book is full of descriptions of birds and birdsong, opening with "the herring gulls on the rail" and ending with "a racket of birdsong, vibrating the air". In between, the poetry spills over with choughs, swallows, herons, magpies and even humans transformed to birds. She's also adept at conjuring city scenes, whether memories of Paris or darker, mysterious portraits of Clydeside ("when a ship's pulling out / to the wailing of horns / all the tenements glide slowly seawards"), and there are vivid glimpses of the townscapes of County Kilkenny where Hardie lives. But it's in her quiet fascination with the sky in all its everyday shape-shifting glory that the work is most at home: "Rain falls all day and it

Gallery Books
*Editor* Peter Fallon
ONLY THIS ROOM

Kerry Hardie

# ONLY THIS ROOM

Gallery Books

*Only This Room*
is first published
simultaneously in paperback
and in a clothbound edition
on 15 October 2009.

The Gallery Press
Loughcrew
Oldcastle
County Meath
Ireland

www.gallerypress.com

ISBN 978 1 85235 480 0 *paperback*
      978 1 85235 481 7 *clothbound*

A CIP catalogue record for this book
is available from the British Library.

# Contents

*for my mother*
*who taught me to read and then fed me with books*

*for Seán*
*without whom there'd be no books of my own*

'I' and 'you' are but the lattices,
In the niches of a lamp,
Through which One Light shines.

'I' and 'you' are the veil
Between heaven and earth;
Lift this veil and you will see
No longer the bond of sects and creeds.

When 'I' and 'you' do not exist,
What is Mosque, what is Synagogue?
What is the Temple of Fire?

— Mahmud Shabistari (died c.1339)

# Gulls in the Morning

The herring gulls on the rail
threaten and swagger and strut.
They rise and alight, they lift up strong beaks,
they ululate into the sky.

I love their cold eyes
and their harsh, headstrong ways.
They call out to something inside me
that is empty and fearless and fierce.

# Earthen

*for Andrew and Tina Kavanagh*

Sometimes when the sky clears
to a thin astonishing blue
the heart turns, looks over its shoulder
at shadows of the tall perennials
cross-hatching an old brick path.
Wind rises.
Dry seed-heads rattle and bow
like old thoughts.
The rivets on a wooden bench
are rusting. Weeds thrive
in cracked and broken bricks
set far below
the clean high sky.
Yet there is beauty
in such fecklessness, such disrepair.
It is our body's native language.

## Unrest

Oh, heart,
why not content yourself
with this beautiful life here on earth?

Why not move through our rooms
like a woman at dusk
and spread a white cloth on our table?

## Old

The flung cries of the choughs,
rags on the windy mountain,
the rattling flight of the magpie,
the heron's flop-winged lift.

And the lambs clamouring the morning,
and the tide rushing the harbour,
and the glamour of hunting kestrel
quartering boggy ground.

# Life is Sweet

*Bus Éireann Expressway*

A man in his middle years walks up the street
holding a wreath in each hand.
The blonde who follows two paces behind
has that worked-over look on her face.
There's a dress shop, Caproni's, offering glitz
for 'All Sizes and All Occasions'.
The bus slows. The boy who stands by the door
stops watching the man with the flowers;
he climbs down and hauls his bag from the hold
while the driver is counting the fare in his hand
and a girl in a narrow coat waits.
Now the driver has started the engine again,
he swings on the wheel and pulls out,
and the girl who's still hanging around in the aisle
staggers and grabs at the back of a seat,
then a youth moves his coat and she sits.

Later, the man with the wreath in each hand
gets drunk and weeps for the uncle who died
and says to the one who's still walking and talking
the things he has worked out alone in the dark
and promised himself that he'll say.
The woman extracts him, drives back through the twilight
and, wearing the dark dress she bought in Caproni's,
lays slices of ham onto bread.
The boy with the bag is mucking out horses,
the driver, long since pulled into the depot,
has phoned home to say he'll be home when he won't,
while the girl who sat by the youth in the bus
has got off in Ennis, his name in her phone,
then waited an hour for her lift.
Her mother, watching the back roads unwind,
thinks she's in better form, but says nothing.

## Reunion

Rain falls all day and it is dark for August.
The sky has wandered off to somewhere else.
Wet petals thin and colour leaches from them,
their fabric curls and folds and smears away.
I watch them in the quietness of thought.
All the loved dead, they come.

## Buried

He said that he'd dreamed that he'd found
something lost years ago, but still longed for.
When he woke he no longer remembered
what it was that had gone, then returned.

The morning lay over the mountain.
A speckled thrush bounced through long grass.

So much light.
When he tried to find where it came from
he searched and there was the dream.

# The Red Window

the red window is open

an island drifts past
on a sea that's as tranquil
as one of those mornings in childhood
which may or may not have existed
in a time that once was
long ago

the island floats off
as you lie there studying the frame
of this window that shatters the wall
as living has shattered your life
letting the light
pour in

## 2

that morning you wake
to find the red window
is full up with weather

a wet thumb has reached
to smudge out the line
where sea changes to sky

and the great waves far out
ride off to the war
while the small waters drip

from the red wooden frame
a sound that is lost
in the wind

# 3

what do we do
at such times —
such times which arrive
unnoticed?

one morning to wake
to the red window frame
a shining day
floating beyond

and the window
is only a window
the red of its frame
only red

and the dog that looks up —
the thump of her tail —
is just an old dog
in the sun

then consolation has gone
and all we can do
is wait without hope
for the things that once spoke

to find voice

# 4

when consolation returns

it plods in the suck of the mud
where the stubborn-haunched cattle
stumble and slide
through the stones of the broken fields

it sits on the green wooden chair
that the dutchman had carried outside
and set down facing the sea
in that hour when the morning still shone —

it blows in the low salt-rain
and seeps in fine drops
from the strands of lank wool
that have snarled on the barbs of the fence

5

*if i die*
*before i wake*

the red window
is bluing with night

*now i lay me*
*with four corners to my bed*

*now i lay me*
*with four angels at my head*

the red window
is bluing

the chant
out of childhood

comes back
like a goodness

that once
long ago

you thought
lay before you

# On the Bus

*after reading Joan Margarit's 'Joana' poems*

These children — damaged, sick or simple.
The girl beside the toilet door in Limerick station,
eight, maybe nine, her dark hair in a *Jeanne d'Arc* helmet,
and how she stood there, smiling, hands held out,
until her mother missed her, came back, told her
it was time to leave the warm air streaming from the dryer.
Then there was the daughter in those poems you wrote:
over and over comes her small hand trusting yours,
comes the misshapen face that you so loved and lost to death.
And now there is this child who sits across from me,
this girl who found my eyes as she moved down the bus,
and I, just waking, thought she'd walked out of the '50s —
the cotton dress, white socks, neat shoes, the hair slide —
her blue eyes, undefended from the stares of strangers.

The dark boy minding her has settled her beside the window
but now she's leaning round to find my eyes again,
her gaze so deep, intense, it's like aggression,
and I have turned away, afraid of seeing what she sees inside me,
afraid that she's unpicking all my closely-seamed deceptions,
until I wonder if she is your daughter come again,
her face all smoothed out and her crutches long discarded,
your daughter come to tell me that misfortune, too,
makes shapes and colours on the life-page, fills it,
and that fear can be accepted, with its deep derangement.
I make myself look back again to find her eyes
but she's elsewhere, this damaged child, her head has fallen
     forward,
her loose-limbed brother sprawls in sleep beside her,
her thick, light hair swings with the bus to veil her.

## Sister Poem

One woman said
*too intense.*
But I wouldn't listen,
had to know better —

Then something happened
and I started looking
out of my left eye.
Nothing was ever the same.

Inside, in a lost garden,
are two still children.
And roses, and roses,
their petals corrupted with earwigs.

# In Galicia

They show him a room that is shadowed and quiet,
the ceiling is high, the cream paint is flaking,
a cavernous wardrobe covers a side wall,
long windows open over the street.

The bed is a boat that is hard, wide and spacious,
its cover, sheened cotton, in broad, heavy stripes.
There's the ochre of scorched sand, the red of set blood,
a green like the Bay of Biscay in storm.

These are the colours he's looked at that morning
in frescoes removed from the walls of a cloister —
white stars on green grounds, figures in togas,
sheep being speared by horned yellow goats.

Unquiet scenes out of *Revelations*.
Nightmares and pledges that once drew all Spain.
Red keyhole arches in gateways from Islam,
great knotted snake-beasts, flattened-out frogs.

He stands and he looks and he knows he's been waiting
all through his life for only this room.
He knows he will nod and turn without entering,
go back down the stairs and hand in his passport,

unpack and stay maybe three days or four
before he will tell them it's time to move on.
He knows he will never get over this leaving,
but sometimes a short time is all we can bear.

# Chipiona

*Spain, mid September*

A woman lies on a folding chair on an empty beach.
Her swimsuit — turquoise — has never known the sea.
Glistening with oil, she offers herself to the sun.

Close by, two men carrying spiked iron tridents
are washing their gear in fresh water that splashes
from the municipal shower.

They are burned by the sun and unshaven.
One is black-haired and the other
has turbaned his head in a T-shirt as green as the sea.

Both men have a dissolute, satisfied air:
the morning has opened, yielding all that it promised,
sliding and silvering out of the shoals of the night.

Now the weather is gathering all along the horizon.
To their right lies the great tidal flow of the Guadalquiver,
above them a gull floats on air that is heavy with myth.

## *Johnny Taylor*

The tenements of Clydeside
were furnished out of liners
built there in the high days.

He filled up his glass,
he said even now,
on a black dirty night,

when a ship's pulling out
to the wailing of horns
all the tenements glide slowly seawards.

## La Vie en Rose

A lame bike is clamped
to a chain's looping sag
like an old dog nobody wants.

It is missing a wheel.
In the shadows indifferent drinkers
are stretched on the pavement and steps.

It is Sunday, and freezing.
Above them, the roofs
of the church of Saint-Étienne

climb the black sky.
Its stained, weary bells
strike forth a vast, hollow sound.

## Osip Mandelstam

Swimming. It's best in the evening.
Best when the fish rise from the depths.

How he could write, it was easy, like swimming.
Once he knew how he couldn't *un*-know.
He took words like 'mother' and 'shadow' and 'linen',
wrote long lines of memory and sorrow and silence,
of violins, young wives (her arms, her white thighs),
of roosters and oxen and stairwells and dresses,
of prisons and black earth and salt-frost and bread,
and far, far away in the depths of the forest
the faint fading hum of Persephone's bees.

Swimming. It's best in the evening.
Best when the day's past, all's lost,
only night lies ahead.

# Coming of Age in the Musée d'Orsay

*for Mick O'Dea*

There's that Cassatt painting I once liked,
a young girl sewing in the summer's green,
her high-necked dress, thinned by the light,
those salmon-pink geraniums, her white skirts.

I pass her by — too wholesome, docile —
or maybe it was all the time I spent
in that strange German book he lent me.
Dix and Beckmann. The black Weimar glitter.

The book     on my bed     all night.

## Exile

Anca,
her bright smock of fraying silk,
writes of the death
of a white cat, frail as a ghost.

*I do not read.*
*I have a hard time*
*just surviving.*

A long time ago,
when her husband had died young,
when her grandmother had died old,
she had defected.

Romania withered inside her.
The white cat has been her companion
all through the stony Paris years.

## Paris Mountains

*for Sheila O'Leary*

The green metal chairs in the Luxembourg Garden
stand around, speaking,
one to another.

In Les Murray's poem the plain young wife
fills a bucket from a stand, then turns to scour
the distant mountains, searching for a city.

In the city you are searching for the mountains.
It is the reason for the loneliness that dwells,
because the mind is looking for its flesh.

But the chairs know nothing of the mountains.
Lacking longing, they continue their discussion.
Lacking loneliness, they have no need of flesh.

# His Teacher

*It is in fact only love that matters, in whatever it may be. They should put out the eyes of painters, as they do those of bull-finches, to make them sing better.*

— Pablo Picasso

In Paris, at the Irish Centre,
the painter in his studio awaits the man
whose portrait he will call 'The Diplomat'.

The diplomat, soaked in his own dreams,
leaves the office in a well-cut suit,
a sweatshirt in Clare colours in his briefcase.

The painter shuts his eyes, a blinded bullfinch,
he sees the sitter's father, once his teacher,
he sees the school, the shops, the town,
the flowery roads, the stone walls flowered with lichen,

and when he finally sets his brushes down
there is a young man, city-dressed, a plain blue ground,
and both the Clare men standing back, astonished,
to see the tender song the bullfinch sang.

## Genesis

If I had it to tell there would still be a garden.
There would be apple trees, leaves wet with rain.
But the walls would be whitethorn, porous and birded:
small spills of song, and the flutter of wings.

And always a wheelbarrow parked by a flowerbed.
And always a rain butt, running black silk.

## That Book

The more you dwell on it
the stranger the situation grows.
Those thieves — they could have been our own.
Hard times. Bones in the wind

on the end of a rope.
Which is why the whole yarn translates so well.
What's as universal as a thief?
A mother. A prostitute. A friend.

Such a long journey
for a story to be travelling.
Odd bits and pieces of talk
blowing out of some desert. Old tribes

wandering about.
Fair winds, foul winds.
Some of their big men tricky.
Some of them straight.

The very same as our own,
dumped for some foreign yarn.
For Davids, Isaacs. For Suzannahs, bathing.
Boyos throwing the leg over somebody else's wife.

We stamped a cross on the sun.
Grafted a cedar onto the ash spreading over the well.
Its waters still ran holy,
still sang of an old, cold bubbling out of the earth.

It's the one between those thieves that's still the problem.
The one who goes on speaking out of turn.
And who knows what he said?
And what they said he said?

*'Do not despair,*
*one of the thieves was saved.*
*Do not presume,*
*one of the thieves was damned.'*

## Winter Morning

*You are here, in this one station, now.*
*This is your portion under the sun.*

This waking in the morning,
the soiled tatters of dream heaping the bed,
this gathering yourself
in the grey dawn.

Over and over
something emerging. Submerging.
So little is conscious. So much
dispossessed.

Being here, in this one station,
in a world
running off into the future,
off into the past.

And our dark prayers
crying themselves.

## Skellig Michael

Wind hones their crosses cut from standing rocks —
stone blades that slice the sunlight, slice the sky.
Weather nips and worries at their walls
that dogged hands re-sculpted against storm.

I've searched for them in texts,
pored over colour plates of books and bells,
of reliquaries for arm-bones, girdles, teeth.
They left no artefacts, no shrines.

What need had they of such?
They were the shrine.
The pattern and the pilgrimage.
The way.

## Strange Company

Someone moved my hands into known holds carved in the rock.
Someone eased my feet into the pocks.
Someone's laughter bubbled in my throat.
Someone's fearlessness erased my fear.

No one climbed the cliff. No one descended.
Everything was as it was, would always be.
Infinity laid out in wind and stone.
The ancient Rule: the wind undoes, the stone defies.

There was a platform, a sea-eagle's scrape.
A seam chipped in bare rock to channel rain.
A ledge that straddled space, creating place.
Blue sheepsbit scabious in the sandy grit.

Someone used my eyes to look.
Someone used my heart to soar.
No one spoke to me of death.
Death belongs with time and time was not.

# Kells Priory

They keep beasts in the cloister,
play handball in the nave,
they sit and pull
on old clay pipes,
tell stories black with filth. Anything
to keep our ghosts at bay.

Piety. Yes, they have that.
But there's a wildness, a quicksilver
men like us could never plumb.
And yet they say the Irish saved
the Light of Christendom —

I lie here in a tomb in a niched arch.
Jackdaws push sticks into a hole
where once a floor-beam lodged.
A starling on the roofless wall
preens high against the sky.

Birds and ghosts. The ruined nave.
Soft, blowy sun in shifting play
upon the floor.

For them the light was outside, not within.
The oratories, the narrow cells,
the stone huts with the doors that framed the sea.

Light is the yearning of their circles on the hills.
Their great tombs mould the darkness
for the spear-pierce of the sun.

To flood the stone with sacred light,
that was our dream. High windows,
and the grace of God within the walls.

The broken nave lies open now,
surrendered to the sky.
Light floods its nests, its lichen-crawls,

its fallen stones.
It lifts the fine lines of the cross
incised upon my tomb —

a cross that bears the likeness of a hilted sword.

## 2 ELIAS, WATCHING SWALLOWS

Last night the rain came. Now the swallows drink,
dipping and splashing in the abbey gutters.

When they've drunk their fill they'll hunker down
and soak heat from the roof-slates in the sun.

When they've warmed and rested in the light
they'll flicker round the cloister, hunting gnats.

When they've done with feeding they'll make busy
dabbing mud-splats in the darkness of the arch.

When they've tired with labouring they'll repeat
the cycle — drinking, warming, feeding — till they breed.

For this reprise their blood has driven their journey:
this cloister in Kilkenny on a morning late in May.

May is God's month. It makes me crave the light,
crave shedding my black armour as the savage knights shed
   theirs —

They shout and stride about until the Reaper wields his scythe,
then buckle on their chain-mail and lie stretched on marble
   tombs.

All creatures have their own lives, their own needs.
Mine is this abbey, all but hidden, like a nest.

A stone church in a hollow place.
A meadowly horizon.

## 3 THE GARDENER'S GRUMBLE

It is January.
Ice-shards in hoof prints. The dark way of silence.
Light lying down on the straw-coloured grasses.
We are cold and ill-tempered but dinner is pig's cheek.
In church they are eating the body of God.

February is Brigit's with spring round the corner
and hard on the spring comes the sweet smell of summer,
three o'clock matins, then dawns wild with birdsong,
and I'm in the garden, shape-changed to a blackbird
grubbing about in the body of God.

# Rebellion

*I am like an elephant: beat me about the head with blows*
*so that I will not dream of India and gardens.*

— Rumi

No blows. I want to dream
of India and gardens. To ignore
the mahout. To set
one great foot after the other. To sway
off into the jungle. To tramp
down to the river and wallow. To spray
shining showers. To live
in joy and pride and disobedience. To lift
my trunk and trumpet the tremendous skies.

# The Valley

*'The first valley is the Valley of the Quest,*
*the second the Valley of Love,*
*the third is the Valley of Understanding,*
*the fourth is the Valley of Independence and Detachment,*
*the fifth of Pure Unity,*
*the sixth is the Valley of Astonishment,*
*and the seventh is the Valley of Poverty and Nothingness*
*beyond which one can go no farther.'*

That is a Sufi story
about a great crowd of birds making ready
to go on an Awful Journey.
They elect the Hoopoe as leader
because he knows a thing or two,
for instance, the lie of the valleys,
and which one comes after which.
What I like is the way it's all more or less as expected
until you arrive at the sixth.

I find myself a bit curious
about this remarkable valley.
I wonder where it lies.
In China, perhaps? In Peru?
I wonder could you stay there
out of your wits with astonishment,
or if, in this witlessness, you might find yourself
stumbling on, over the mountain —

## Humankind

We carry the trust.
It was not imposed on us,
nor are we heedless.

Sometimes the stillness stands in the woods
and lies on the lake. We move like drowned beings
through clouded waters.

Sometimes we wake to spent leaves
blowing about in the yard. A door bangs.
A woman — vigorous — shakes a rug into the wind.

The red dog shudders and rises and listens.
Uncertain light shines the grasses.
Wealth sits in inner rooms, staring.

These are our days.
Walk them.
Fear nothing.

# Great Northern Divers in Ballinskelligs Bay

*after meeting the Catalan poet, Joan Margarit, in Galway*

Now, by the sea,
feet in the sea,
and the waves
washing over them.
Watching these birds,
birds with the cry
of a wolf that's made mad
by the moon —

and the sea here so still and so pale
and the black and white birds swimming low,
half submerged and ambling about
on the ghost-grey stillness of water
like two people walking and talking
as we did that night, in the long northern light —

and I think now how simple
was simple desire,
how when I was young
I fell down into love
with every man
that I slept with —
while now I just fall into love
with the way a whole life has been lived
inside a body not young anymore,
not quick, not fine,
but thickened with all the lived life —

there are people you know for a day
and you love them and all their lived lives
and the way you can swim with them out onto water
so still and so pale that it hardly exists

except as a luminous ground
for this drifting, this talking —

but now the divers have plunged,
no trace marks the swell
lying under the shift of sea-light.

## Gannets

The ink-dipped tips
of their ivory wings,
their cruciform shape
laid flat on the sea.

Yet sometimes my boot
finds a wreckage of bird
part-smothered in wrack
and a silting of sand,

dun-grey and fine,
bones pushing through,
and small crawling things
*world-without-end-amen.*

## Once

There were roofs on these walls
men and women
children          voices

Lambs stumble about
in the sea-fret
bleating        bleating

such sounds
            as are owned
by the world

# September Thoughts

*after reading Follain*

She squats in the matted woods making water
into the moss and the hush, vague with gnats;
stares at the silvery trail of the slug
round the tea-brown, contorted, inedible fungi —
while up in the house they sit waiting and knowing
that this time is always like this —
                              is always suspended
centuries deep, and will pass — the trees
will open their hands and the shores of the lake
will clot with drowned leaves; the people will dream
and die and give birth and hoard money.
Everything will go on going on, she has only
to lie on the floor reading books.
Already the darkness presses the window.

## Helplessness

Oh, heart,
why can't you learn
that there is nothing to do in the world except live in it?

Why can't you take its deep gifts —
the birds and the cars in the rain;
lost keys and the broken-hearted?

## Samhain

You can feel the dead crowding.
In the fierce, low sun they've kept their distance:
light-fade and they flock like small brown moths
that dart and fall and crawl and rise and settle,
cloaking my shoulders with their soft, drab wings.

The great saints have their high appointed ritual.
This is a congregation of the parish dead,
local to these scattered fields and farms.

# Remembering His Birthday

*November*

Up on the hill,
the sky spitting rain,
a spaniel covering ground;

these dates that lay tracks
through the field of the mind
like the trail of a hare on damp grass.

# Sanctuary

A swallow-built mud nest inside the porch.
They've laid eggs, reared young,
flicked around the skies till late September.

Then bats moved in, came pouring out
to hunt the half-light. The world slid into darkness
and they sought a deeper roost.

One night I stood there, talking to a neighbour.
Some movement tripped the light beside the nest —
the sudden brightness woke a thread of wrens.

We counted twelve.
They must have crowded tight against the cold,
a feathered ball of fiercely living lives.

Heart, I said, could you do that? Become a place of stillness?
Immune from me and emptied of my passions
a mud-cup shelter, lined with hair and down?

Heart heard me but it didn't answer.
It was intent on its own business
which I had blundered into when the light came on.

# Slant

A dark thought, to go swimming so late in the year, the rain
trying to come. A dark thing to do — no one about, the stillness
I'd seen in the woods making shapes by the shoreline.

The tall weeds: sowthistle, willowherb, hogweed —
their great stalks, their seed-heads, their few withered leaves —
all standing sentinel, stripped back to bone-life.

Small birds at the water's edge, *chip-chips* of panic. A small wind
shivering the last leaves, shivering the lake, which was black
from the hanging sky, black in the silence,

while out in the water the lipping and lapping,
the deep fishes brushing, their dense supple forms.
Then the thought, *If I thought*

*that I couldn't swim back, then I couldn't swim back.*
That morning at breakfast he'd listened and nodded,
reached for the jug, set it down, and remarked

that it's hard to like someone
if you don't like them —
or maybe she said it, I don't remember, sometimes

it isn't who speaks words as long as they're spoken
and lie there like air lying down on the water.
Thinking this, I forgot about not swimming back.

I swam back.

# Marriage

*for Roisin Lonergan*

You see, I remember your childhood,

remember walking away
from that house one June night,
late,
the light blue, you children asleep,
and I, turning round, looking back
at the white birds your mother had called,
white birds like magnolia flames,
to float and dream over that house
all through the short summer darkness,
the long winter darkness,
so fierce her resolve
that it summoned this gentleness.

So what is it like now to leave,
to walk through the door and away?

I know that a hundred years on
you'll still sleep in this house,
through the summer's short night,
will still open morning eyes to the light,
and a fading drift of white birds —

# Grief

*for Anne, October '07*

Everything trivial
is erased.

It is being alone
on a high place of moorland or mountain

with the howl of the wind, and the fool,
scrambling on all fours, whimpering,

somewhere below and behind you,
desperate to comfort,

to keep up —

## Thirty Years

These days there is only a silence between us.
All the shoving and pushing, the sound and the fury,
have stilled. I wake in your arms with the silence.
We lie there inside it, not sleeping, not speaking.
Outside, a racket of birdsong, vibrating the air.

# Acknowledgements and Notes

Acknowledgements are due to the editors of the following magazines and periodicals where some of these poems, or versions of them, were published first: *The Clifden Anthology, Cúirt Journal, Heat, The Missouri Review, Poetry Ireland Review, THE SHOp, The Stinging Fly, The Warwick Review, Weyfarers* and *Upstairs at Duroc.*

The author wishes to thank the Tyrone Guthrie Centre at Annaghmakerrig and Kilkenny County Council for a bursary to cover the residency; the Cill Rialaig Project; Grellan Rourke and Alan Hayden for their knowledge, patience and hospitality on Skellig Michael; Helen Carey and the Centre Culturel Irlandais, Paris, for time there as Writer in Residence; Alan Counihan and the 'Sculpture at Kells Committee' for the invitation to write about Kells Priory; and last but not least the staff of Graiguenamanagh Library for their invaluable help in sourcing books.

*page* 10 This quotation comes from a text called *The Secret Rose Garden* (Gulshan-i Raz) written about 1311.

*page* 23 Joan Margarit's daughter Joana was born with severe damage to the brain and spine. He wrote both poems and prose about her birth, life and death. 'Joana knew that her survival depended on the affection of those around her and she learned straightaway that affection alone generates affection . . . Joana's end, thirty years later, was devasting' (*Barcelona Amor Final*, translated by Anna Crowe).

*page* 25 The frescoes referred to are in the Monasterio de Santo Toribio de Liébana in Northern Spain.

*page* 35 Samuel Beckett claimed the quotation used in the last stanza as St Augustine's, though the words themselves can't be found in any of the saint's surviving works.

*page* 38 Sometime in the 12th century the anchorite monks left the Monastery of Skellig Michael. A new monastery was built on the shores of Ballinskelligs Bay and the Augustinian rule was adopted. The Augustinians were a reforming order, originally drawn from mother houses in Britain. Their brief was to regularize the Celtic

Church in Britain and Ireland. Thus the old monastic settlements were replaced by the great continental orders, though occasionally relics and artefacts survived from an earlier age. None was found on Skellig Michael.

page 39   A hermitage is situated high up on the south peak of Skellig Michael. It cannot be seen from the monastery itself, or from below, and was clearly designed as a station of solitude for a single hermit. It is reached now with difficulty, but the vertiginous path has ancient hand- and foot-holds cut into vertical rock by the monks.

page 40   Kells Priory is a ruined Augustinian Foundation in County Kilkenny. Until the 14th century the priors were all appointed from the mother house in Cornwall.

page 42   Elias of Shortallstown was the first Irish Prior of Kells. The Augustinians wore black robes. The Norman knights who held sway in Kilkenny were buried under their effigies, carved from the local black marble.

page 43   Augustinian monks, all fully ordained priests, used servants and labourers for all manual tasks including the vegetable garden.

page 45   The first stanza is quoted from *The Conference of the Birds* by Farid ud-Din Attar, written in the second half of the 12th century. This rendering into English is by C S Nott (Samuel Weiser, 1969).